No. 4 **Gray Barker's Newsletter** Feb. 1976

Gray Barker

Gray Baker's Newsletter
No. 4, Feb. 1976

Gray Baker
Alfred Steber (Editor)

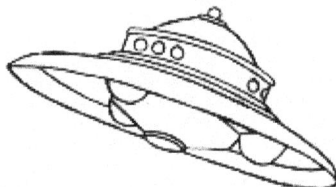

SAUCERIAN PUBLISHER
Original Sources in Ufology

ISBN: 978-1-955087-41-4

9 781955 087414

2022, Saucerian Publisher

PROLOGUE

It is generally a good idea to return to the classics in any genre. This also goes for UFO literature. Rereading a book, or reviewing old documents after ten or twenty years is a rewarding experience. You will discover new data and ideas you didn´t notice before. The reason, of course, is that you are, in many ways, not the same person reading the book the second or third time. Hopefully you have advanced in knowledge, experience, intellectual and spiritual discernment. A good starting point is to reread the UFO classics in order to understand the deeper mystery involved in what happened during that era.

Gray Baker's Newsletter was a leading forum for personal experiences relating to UFOs, psychic abilities, ghosts and hauntings, cryptozoology, alternative medicine, and Fortean phenomena for a devoted readership worldwide. This title is an authentic reproduction of the *Gray Baker's Newsletter* for February, 1976. Great, but unpretentious, this issue is an extraordinarily rare symbol of what was going on in those early years of the modern UFO phenomena. Cover illustration of John Keel surrounded by his "Eight Towers" denizens.

Saucerian Publisher was founded with the mission of promoting books in Science Fiction. Our vision is to preserve the legacy of literary history by reprint editions of books which have already been exhausted or are difficult to obtain. Our goal is to help readers, educators and researchers by bringing back original publications that are difficult to find at reasonable price, while preserving the legacy of universal knowledge. This book is an authentic reproduction of the original printed text in shades of gray. **IMPORTANT**, despite the fact that we have attempted to accurately maintain the integrity of the original work, the present reproduction may have minor errors beyond our control like: missing and blurred pages, poor pictures and readers' pencil markings from the original scanned copy. Because this book is culturally important, we have made available as part of our commitment to protect, preserve and promote knowledge in the world.

This book has been formatted from their original version for publication. **IMPORTANT, although we have attempted to maintain the integrity of the issues accurately, the present reproduction could have blurred pages and poor pictures due to the age of the original scanned copy.**

Editor
Saucerian Publisher

Flying Saucer Investigator Gray Barker (May 2, 1925 – December 6, 1984)

Grayson R Barker

in the U.S., Find a Grave Index, 1600s-Current

GRAY R BARKER
MAY 2, 1925
DEC 6, 1984

Want to get involved? Click here.

ⓘ Report a problem

Detail Source

Name:	Grayson R Barker
Gender:	Male
Birth Date:	2 May 1925
Birth Place:	Braxton County, West Virginia, United States of America
Death Date:	6 Dec 1984
Death Place:	Braxton County, West Virginia, United States of America
Cemetery:	Barker Cemetery
Burial or Cremation Place:	Sutton, Braxton County, West Virginia, United States of America
Has Bio?:	Y
Father:	George Elliott Barker
Mother:	Rosa Lee Barker

REGISTRATION CARD (Men born on or after July 1, 1924, and on or before December 31, 1924)

(Also for the registration of men as they reach the 18th anniversary of the date of their birth on or after January 1, 1943.)

SERIAL NUMBER	1. NAME (Print)			ORDER NUMBER
W 159	Gray	Roscoe	Barker	11,688
	(First)	(Middle)	(Last)	

2. PLACE OF RESIDENCE (Print)

	Riffle	Braxton	W. Va.
(Number and street)	(Town, township, village, or city)	(County)	(State)

[THE PLACE OF RESIDENCE GIVEN ON LINE 2 ABOVE WILL DETERMINE LOCAL BOARD JURISDICTION; LINE 2 OF REGISTRATION CERTIFICATE WILL BE IDENTICAL]

3. MAILING ADDRESS

Glenville, Gilmer Co., W. Va.

(Mailing address if other than place indicated on line 2. If same, insert word same.)

4. TELEPHONE	5. AGE IN YEARS 18	6. PLACE OF BIRTH Riffle
	DATE OF BIRTH May 2 1925	(Town or county) W. Va.
(Exchange) (Number)	(Mo.) (Day) (Yr.)	(State or country)

7. NAME AND ADDRESS OF PERSON WHO WILL ALWAYS KNOW YOUR ADDRESS

Mr. G. E. Barker, Riffle, W. Va. (father)

8. EMPLOYER'S NAME AND ADDRESS

None

9. PLACE OF EMPLOYMENT OR BUSINESS

(Number and street or R. F. D. number)	(Town)	(County)	(State)

I AFFIRM THAT I HAVE VERIFIED ABOVE ANSWERS AND THAT THEY ARE TRUE.

DSS Form 1 (Rev. 11-16-43)   16—21630-4   (OVER)

Gray Barker
(Registrant's signature)

Gray Barker (May 2, 1925-December 6, 1984)

Tthe most famous UFOlogist in history , and flying saucer investigator who was the leading figures among flying saucer researchers, who hase challenged the government denial that saucers come from outer space, have been silenced, Gray Roscoe Barker (May 2, 1925-December 6, 1984) was born in Riffle, Braxton County. He grew up in Braxton County and spent most of his life in central West Virginia. After receiving a B.A. from Glenville State College in 1947, he taught school and became a booking agent for theaters in the area.

In 1952, he was working as a theater booker in Clarksburg, West Virginia, when he began collecting stories about the Flatwoods Monster, an alleged extraterrestrial reported by residents of nearby Braxton County. Barker submitted an article about the creature to FATE Magazine and shortly afterward began writing regular pieces about UFOs for Space Review, a magazine published by Albert K. Bender's International Flying Saucer Bureau.

In 1953, Albert K. Bender abruptly dissolved his organization, claiming that he could not continue writing about UFOs because of "orders from a higher source". After pressing Bender for more details, Barker wrote his first book, They Knew Too Much About Flying Saucers, published by University Books in 1956.[4] The book was the first[3] to describe the Men in Black, a group of mysterious figures who, according to UFO conspiracy theorists, intimidate individuals into keeping silent about UFOs. Barker recounted Bender's alleged encounters with the Men in Black, who were said to travel in groups of three, wear black suits, and drive large black automobiles, usually Cadillacs. In 1962, Barker and Bender collaborated on a second book entitled: Flying Saucers and the Three Men. Published under Barker's imprint, Saucerian Books, this book proposed that the Men in Black were extraterrestrials.

Barker published his best-known book, They Knew Too Much About Flying Saucers, in 1956. At various times Barker published flying saucer magazines and newsletters. Through these publications, he contacted people worldwide interested in UFOs, many of whom claimed to have been contacted by aliens.

Over the following decades, Barker continued writing books about UFOs and other paranormal phenomena. In 1970, following the 1967 collapse of the Silver Bridge in Point Pleasant, Barker published his next book, The Silver Bridge. This publication is related to the famous legend of the Mothman sightings. Although he published many other books on strange phenomena, Barker is best known for these two books and a 1983 publication called MIB, The Terror Among Us, about the Men in Black. He was the subject of the 1995 video by Ralph Coon, Whispers From Space. For this production, Coon collected stories from various people who knew and worked with Barker.

Though his books advocated the existence of UFOs and extraterrestrials, Barker was privately skeptical of the paranormal. His sister Blanch explained that Barker only wrote the books for the money, and his friend James W. Moseley said Barker "pretty much took all of UFOlogy as a joke". In a letter to John C. Sherwood, who had submitted materials to Saucerian Books as a teenager, Barker referred to his paranormal writings as his "kookie books."

Barker occasionally engaged in deliberate hoaxes to deceive UFO enthusiasts. In 1957, for example, Barker and Moseley wrote a fake letter (signed "R.E. Straith") to self-claimed "contactee" George Adamski, telling Adamski that the United States Department of State was pleased with Adamski's research into UFOs. The letter was written on State Department stationery, and Barker himself described it as "one of the great mysteries of the UFO field" in his 1967 Book of Adamski.

According to Sherwood's Skeptical Inquirer article "Gray Barker: My Friend, the Myth-Maker", there may have been "a grain of truth" to Barker's writings on the Men in Black, in that the United States Air Force and other government agencies did attempt to discourage public interest in UFOs during the 1950s. However, Barker is thought to have greatly embellished the facts of the situation. In the same Skeptical Inquirer article, Sherwood revealed that, in the late 1960s, he and Barker collaborated on a brief fictional notice alluding to the Men in Black, published as fact first in Raymond A. Palmer's Flying Saucers magazine and some of Barker's publications. In the story, Sherwood (writing as "Dr. Richard H. Pratt") claimed he was ordered to silence by the "black men" after learning that UFOs were time-traveling vehicles. Barker later wrote to Sherwood, "Evidently, the fans swallowed this one with a gulp."

Gray Barker's fame spread after his death in 1984 at age 59. A 1995 video by Ralph Coon recognized Barker as one of the 20th century's leading UFO theorists. Barker's collection is now part of the Clarksburg-Harrison Public Library. When asked once if he believed in flying saucers, Barker replied, "I am not sure, but anything that generates that volume of interest is worth collecting."

ABOVE: Artist Gene Duplantier pictures John Keel surrounded by the denizens of his Superspectrum discussed in The Eighth Tower (See Book Review). Keel believes that these creatures are real and solid but materialize and dematerialize here by a complex process. If you are a serious UFO buff you may be able to identify by name all of the Visitors pestering the author as he tries to read the current SKYLOOK in this non-too-serious treatment -- and if you can do so we will reward you with two knocks on the head.

2

The Great Phonograph In the Sky

THE INVISIBLE COLLEGE, by Jacques Vallee, E. P. Dutton & Co., Inc., New York, 1976, 216 pages, $8.95.

THE EIGHTH TOWER, by John A. Keel, Saturday Review Press/E. P. Dutton & Co., Inc., New York, 1976, 218 pages, $8.95.

It is unusual that two UFO books, in many ways so similar, should come out (from essentially the same publisher since Sat. Review Press evidently is a subsidiary of Dutton) only a few days apart (TOWER Jan. 29, COLLEGE Jan. 15), and yet be different enough that each may represent an important contribution to saucer literature. Although, to the average reader, these represent heady doses of new ideas, neither is a bolt out of the blue: TOWER had an excellent introduction in Keel's OPERATION TROJAN HORSE, while COLLEGE was preceded seven years ago by a somewhat radical book (for a nuts and bolts scientist), Vallee's haunting PASSPORT TO MAGONIA, in which the author connected saucers with mythology and folklore.

Both books are by authors with greatly different backgrounds: Keel is a gifted journalist with no academic credentials to our knowledge, but with years of experience in professional writing that only in recent years was employed in saucer reporting. He has a staunch sentiment for Middle Ufology, connections and friendship with the Eastern UFO Establishment personalities. Keel, who once did a radio broadcast from Frankenstein's castle (it actually exists!) got into radical Ufology with HORSE, and it is not surprising that TOWER, his latest, should take us further into some mind-wrenching extra-dimensions. As usual, he brings it off with skill, persuasion and a well-needed chuckle or two.

Vallee, on the other hand, should be the traditional academician, confining his writing to papers and books that conform to the strictures of scholarly publication. French in origin, Vallee earned his master's degree in astrophysics in France, and his Ph. D. in computer science, while an associate of J. Allen Hynek at Northwestern University. While not as bold in his speculations as is Keel, the French author in COLLEGE successfully crosses the barrier into pure Middle Ufology, a Great Gulf (for a scientist) more forminable than the eye of a needle for a camel. Though no doubt influenced and encouraged by Hynek, Vallee has apparently struck out on his own into Ufological pastures into which his mentor (at least publicly) has not dared to graze.

But while Keel lunges into these dreaded fields astride his fabulous Trojan Horse, which he sneaked in past saucer buffs who were still looking through telescopes for ET's, Vallee enters on a far grander steed. It is a horse with wings; his Pegasus is plainly showing. It is almost as if the Prince and the Pauper have met and exchanged their habits: Keel donning the black robe of a scientific explainer, Vallee appropriating the rags of a poet in his search for meaning. His approach in COLLEGE, with ideas and theories not clearly stated, makes the book difficult for me to review to my satisfaction and the reader's own persusal is highly recommended -- for I may have penetrated one of its levels and missed another.

To deal with these two books in separate reviews could lead to considerable redundancy; together they make more sense as a whole, and a case against the extraterrestrial hypothesis that is convincing. This marks the first time that one of our publications has reviewed two books together, and the first time a book review has been given front cover and lead story prominence. I hope this will tend to indicate the importance we ascribe to these books.

GRAY BARKER'S NEWSLETTER is an official publication of the Saucers and Unexplained Celestial Events Research Society (SAUCERS). Published irregularly. 6 issues $6.00. By domestic first class mail $7.00. By foreign air mail $12.00. Exchanges with other zines. Published by Saucerian Press, Inc., Box 2228, Clarksburg, WV 26301 U.S. Clippings and other saucerinformation needed.

     The word "spectre" comes from the Greek word for "spectrum,"
deriving from the ancients' observations that weird apparitions often
came into view while associated with a dark red color, and made their
exits in ultra violet hue. This offers Keel a key to endow his Ufonauts
(a term he used often in HORSE) with some scientific basis and respecta-
bility though they exist in another dimension. First developed in HORSE,
Keel carries his idea of creatures and things outside our visible spectrum
further, and devises what he terms a Superspectrum (See back cover).
Of course Keel, with his ingratiating and convincing writing style, probably
could tell us that Richard Hall just became a card carrying member of
AFSCA and make us believe it. I can't quite understand all of his charts
and diagrams, particularly one large circular graph that fills a whole page,
but still he makes a lot of sense in a general way. Keel, at least, gives
us something "concrete" that the average layman can argue about, while
Vallee waxes just a bit too philosophical for us to corner. With Keel a
journalist and Vallee a scientist, this is the antithesis of what should
be, and poses another contrast between these similar works.
     Keel begins with a scientific discussion that is universally accepted:
The Audio Spectrum, consisting of vibrations that our ears can hear, begins
with the borderland of low frequency hearing (Infrasonic/Bass) at 16 cycles
per second, progresses upward through the treble range, and ends at about
20,000 cycles for most people, where sound enters the ultrasonic range
(many animals can hear sounds somewhat above this range, which may account
for their strange behavior during or before/after the appearance of unusual
phenomena). From this point we enter the Electromagnetic Spectrum beginning
with VLF (very low frequency) radio, to conventional broadcast radio into
short wave; from VHF (very high frequency) to Microwave.
     Concentrated microwaves in an oven cooks many of our TV dinners and
is a suspected source of the adverse physical effects suffered by some UFO
witnesses. From microwaves the next step upward on the Electromagnetic
Spectrum is heat, at the border of the Infra-red, or the beginning of visible
light. As the frequencies increase we go through the colors of the rainbow,
ending in Ultra-violet and in invisibility -- the end of the range of
human seeing (though Keel believes many people, particularly those psychic-
ally gifted, can see slightly beyond and/or below this average range of
sight perception).
     From this point Keel takes us still farther, and still on commonly-
accepted ground. From the Ultra-violet we go into even higher frequencies,
the world of X-rays, Gamma rays, and Cosmic rays, in that order.
     To find the lair of the Ufonauts, however, Keel proposes a continu-
ation of the accepted spectrum, which he dubs the Superspectrum. It is
from this vast area of pseudo-comprehensibility from which emerge the
motley throng of saucermen, hairy monsters, MIB, as well as all the other
puzzling "unreal" things that have confronted man ever since his beginning.
Such "creatures" can, either through some ability of the human being to
materialize them, or by their own wills, alter their rates of vibration
or frequencies, and emerge into our visible and even audible spectra.
     During such materializations the saucers (a broad term I use here to
represent all of the phenomena) may draw physical substance from the
earthly environment to make themselves solid, including the abundant sulphur
in our polluted atmosphere), and other elements such as silicon. After a
short "life span" on Earth they dematerialize, often dumping the earthly
construct material. While some of them, like Old Soldiers, may "just
fade away," Keel notes that in some cases, "The poor slobs just melt away,"
often leaving unpleasant odors.
     The huge, unpleasant hairy creatures, and other critters seen in
connection with UFO flaps become logical within Keel's reasoning. After
all, nobody has caught an Abominable Snowman, a Bigfoot, a Mothman or the
Loch Ness Monster (which Keel believes is the same sort of construct).
Yet these things do seem to be real, and the "dinosaurs" and "hairy monsters"

do leave huge tracks, demonstrating creatures of considerable weight. In the case of the hairy monsters Keel logically observes that huge creatures of the size and weight reported would consume a lot of food if staying around, and exhaust a huge number of farm animals in a short period -- yet there seems to be only isolated incidents of killed or missing animals during such monster flaps (the cattle mutilations seem to involve a different set of circumstances). This is because the "hairy monsters" do not stay around very long. In fact their sickening odor, almost a common denominator of "monster" sightings, and associated with demonaic appearances in the past, may be "rotten egg gas" or hydrogen sulphide, one of the products of the already hastening decomposition of these "creatures" when they are seen.

But just who are the saucerpeople, and why are they doing all this? On this subject Keel seems to be getting less certain as he goes from book to book. In HORSE he gave me the impression that he believed these to be intelligent entities, or maybe even gods of some sort, and that they were materializing in the form that could be acceptable to the intellectual frame of reference of the witness. My impression is that both Keel and Vallee are "graduating" from the anecdotal process of reporting weird sightings and are searching for further meanings. If they engage in monologues it may be to straighten their own heads, not the readers'. But these forays into the philosophical makes for some good quotes. Like the Christian god, who stayed to dwell within us after the ascension of Christ, Keel suggests that the gods of the ancients have returned. "But they do not come to us from across the chasm of interstellar space. They come somehow from within us. They have always been faceless, because their faces are our faces reflected in the superspectrum." Is our conscious existence a macabre charade of imagined existence, and is the Superspectrum itself the only reality? This, Keel suggests. "The rest......is something we have manufactured in our own madness and our lonely, painful search for meaning."

Although Vallee, like Donald H. Menzel, has also written science fiction (Vallee received a Jules Verne Prize for his first sci-fi novel written in French), Keel is not such an author to my knowledge (though he has written under different pseudonyms). In TOWER, however, the reader must seperate an occasional sci-fi extrapolation from what he is actually saying or trying to express.

THE EIGHTH TOWER gets its title from a description in a William Seabrook fantasy/adventure novel, of seven towers located throughout the world, which were inhabited by seven devils, which, in effect, ruled the world. Keel proposes an eighth tower, though a somewhat fictional one. It is reminiscent of one of Vallee's actual cases, that of an engineer who vanished for several days while he absorbed information from a huge unattended computer which played various recordings to him. The engineer acquired psychic abilities and experienced an almost complete life change. Keel envisions a computer of sorts, probably housed in the Superspectrum. It could have been constructed by an ancient race of Titans or super-beings who created humans and enslaved them, controlling their existences completely. When the earth suffered many cataclysms, the super-race departed, neglecting to turn off their complex device. For a while this computer still was able to largely control human existence, through the traditional "divine right" of kings. With the industrial revolution, the deification of technology (and the rise of the Invisible College of olden days), mankind gradually began to break away from this enslavement.

Though parted personally from their Cosmic Masters whom they once served and worshipped as gods, all humans, some more than others, are still in various stages of contact with the great "computer," or Keel's EIGHTH TOWER.

"It is almost as if some giant phonograph in the sky has been patiently playing the same record over and over again for centuries.

        "I think the stage is set for the appearance of new faiths, centered
on the UFO belief," states Vallee in THE INVISIBLE COLLEGE. "To a greater
degree than all the phenomena modern science is confronting, the UFO can
inspire awe, the sense of the smallness of man, and an idea of the possibility of contact with the cosmic." As already suggested, the absence of
clear-cut dogma in COLLEGE makes it a difficult task to review and especially to digest into any specific mold. The author will have to forgive
me if we pick out the quotation above to represent a dominant theme.

        And of course a major idea in COLLEGE is the rejection of the extra-
terrestrial hypothesis: Vallee's saucers certainly are certainly not from
outer space (although they might be from "inner space"). And of course
they have always been around: "In antiquity their occupants were regarded
as gods; in medieval times, as magicians; in the nineteenth century,
scientific geniuses. And finally, in our own time, as interplanetary
travelers." Peter Kor will turn over in his Tom Comella shroud when he
hears his esoteric jargon published in English by a Frenchman.

        During the Dark Ages scientists pursued their studies in secrecy.
The Alchemists (and before them, of course, the witches) were the precursors
of today's scientists. Hidden away in their laboratories and studies,
these early scientists formed what has been termed an "Invisible College,"
secretly working and communicating with each other beneath the intellectual
surface of the times.

        Vallee believes that in some ways the present time has been appropriate
for the formation of a modern Invisible College, an informal association of
about 100 scientists all over the world. Like their counterparts of old,
who lived in fear of the ruling intellectual authority, members of this age
have seldom dared to attack the UFO mystery to avoid persecution by their
fellow academicians. In case the reader may feel that Vallee is being too
dramatic, I refer you to the sufferings of Immanuel Velikovsky at the hands
of his colleagues.

        Although Vallee does not name examples, we can assume that Hynek
has been a member (though we doubt that Menzel ever enrolled). Working
in secret, these scientists have given discreet support to groups of ama-
teurs who have assembled the data that could not be obtained through official channels, and have safeguarded these valuable resources. He suggests
that the time is right for the College to surface, as it did at the end
of the Dark Ages when the Royal Society was formed. In both his earlier
PASSPORT TO MAGONIA and in COLLEGE Vallee seems to be ascending from
this secret campus in a massive trial balloon. So far he has not been shot
down, and the air in his vessel of intellectual levitation , like the
author's personality, has remained pretty cool.

        Although COLLEGE is a book of _ideas_, the author illustrates these
with a wide selection of cases (both Keel and he cite some of the same).
One of his most fascinating disclosures which I previously had never heard
about, is the existence of a Spanish group known as UMMO, which gained
prominence during 1970 and 1971. This group claims communication with
outer space, from saucerians residing on a planet that circles Wolf 424.
These communications collected by UMMO followers contain surprisingly
accurate technical and mathematical information, particularly in regard
to the position of their home planet, all checked out by scientists who
found the figures difficult to disprove. The Spanish government became
interested in these documents, despite the "extraterrestrials'" request
that the information not be given to government officials. Even in France
when the U.S. Air Force was closing down Project Bluebook, high officials
were impressed by UMMO, and had done their own research on it with the help
of French scientists. These scientists had concluded that "in order to
shoot down the UMMO theory one needs, astronomically speaking, very strong
arguments." Although Vallee suggests that UMMO could possibly have been
the result of an experiment in the training of intelligence personnel,
either by the Spanish government or by some foreign agency, the name of

6

JACQUES VALLEE

"the maddening simplicity
of unattended clockwork"

of which might begin with
a "C", it remains one of
the most puzzling cases
in his book.

In a chapter, "The
Morphology of Miracles," he
relates the experiences of
Joseph Smith, who founded
Mormonism, and this becomes
one more corollary of the
so-called "saucer visi-
tations" of today. Smith
was visited by radiant
beings who told him of the
existence of gold plates
containing text he should
translate. Several wit-
nesses actually saw the
plates at the time they were being translated by a kind of "key" left by
the shining beings. This remarkable translation became The Book of Mormon,
the sacred text of the new faith, which outlined the visitation of Jesus
Christ to the Americas, and the appearance of Christ's apostles in the
form of Nephi, which had appearances in some ways similar to the modern
Men In Black.

Although sightings of UFOs have been inextricably linked with so-
called religious phenomena throughout the ages, cases such as Joseph
Smith are rarities, however, since only a small number of such
"contactees" catch human imagination and are able to initiate and lead
major religious movements.

Those who, although they have not started new movements, have
gained large followings within the framework of an existing faith, include
Bernadette of Lourdes, and the three children visited by the Blessed Virgin
Mary. The latter predicted a public display which became the famous
Miracle of Fatima. The circumstances leading to the Miracle and the
Miracle itself are well described and documented by Vallee. Although
this has been pursued by many authors, Vallee succeeds best in placing
it within the UFO framework.

And Vallee partly assauges our curiosity about the message left
with the children by the BVM (his abbreviation for Blessed Virgin Mary),
though it is still hearsay. A trusted friend of the author told him that
he had the report from one of the Pope's secretaries, who introduced high
churchmen into the presence of John XXII for the 1960 opening. Although
the secretary was not allowed to be present in the room with the Pope
and churchmen, he noted "a look of deep horror on their faces" as they
left the pontiff's office. He tried to detain one of the Cardinals whom
he knew intimately, but was gently pushed aside as the prelate hurriedly
exited "with the expression of someone who had seen a ghost." Did the
prophecy, by any chance, have anything to do with the modern UFO phenomena?
We can only guess.

At any rate these religious phenomena may also have sociological
significance, for as the author points out, France at the end of the 19th
century and Portugal in 1917 were about to experience "social and
political turning points, deeply influencing the collective psyche."
The appearances of the BVM seemed to herald these events.

The nearest to a concrete theory Vallee offers is probably his
Control System. The UFOs and allied phenomena are controlling our
thoughts and subjecting us to a continuing educational program, whether
for good or bad. Their coming in regular "waves" or "flaps" conforms to a
recognized pedagogical process which recognizes that a continuous teaching
process dulls the mind, but that interruptions in the process tends to
reinforce learning and to make it unforgetable. Should we continue a

scientific investigation of UFOs to learn more about this Control System?
Definitely, he believes, but we should also devote more attention to "the
shift in our world view that the phenomena produces," or, in other words,
how it is affecting mankind. Vallee sees it as the evolution of a new
religion which will try to cope with troubled times ahead. Should one
step aboard blindly and go along with it? He isn't sure.

Of the members of the Establishment now venturing into the treacher-
ous realm of Middle Ufology, with all of its hidden quagmires -- and its
oases of intellectual challenge and satisfaction, we like Vallee the most
and believe, that like T'sain in Jack Vance's fictional The Dying Earth,
he has committed to mind enough spells to survive the ravages of the
Mazarians. And he will be no slave to the Control System he may have
intellectually invented (or perhaps even to the systemization we Ufologists
have tried to impose):

"I would like to step outside the conditioning maze and see what
makes it tick," he says. He is well aware of the perils he might
encounter there in his tortured turmoil. Among his most feared might
be "the maddening simplicity of unattended clockwork."

Answers to the UFO riddle, he feels, cannot be provided by scientists, or in some secret file in Washington. The solution is ours to reach
any time we want it.

"The solution lies where it has always been: within ourselves."
                                        -- Gray Barker

===

THE STRANGE EXPERIENCES OF A SALEM FAMILY
Investigated and Reported by Mark Swift

The following incidents took place in Salem, Ohio, a small community
near Youngstown. The witnesses are sincere in their convictions and I
found them credible.

One morning in the Spring of 1968 about 10:00 A.M. Mrs. Alice J.
Allison was looking out the window when she noticed a strange object.
"It looked like an airplane without wings," she said. She described it
as totally black and without lights. She thought the object had an engine
because it made a very strange noise. "It sounded like a helicopter," she
told me, "but it had no propellers." The craft was hovering over her
buckeye tree, which was about 30 feet high. She could see an occupant
clearly because the front portion of the craft was covered with a clear
dome.

I asked her to describe the occupant. "He was a 'man' and he wore a
khaki colored shirt. He had an olive colored skin, which was slightly
tanned, and his eyes were slanted." She thought the occupant was worried
because the craft was sputtering and rocking back and forth in the air, as
if it had engine trouble. The sighting continued for about 20 minutes
and finally the object left in the direction of the southwest at a slow rate
of speed. I talked with her son, Bruce, who is 14 (7 or 8 at the time of
the sighting) and he described the craft similarly except he did not see
the occupant because he viewed the object from the rear.

Although there is the remote possibility that a helicopter could have
been misinterpreted as a UFO, subsequent events do seem to fit a "pattern"
often reported by witnesses after a "saucer" sighting.

Ever since the sighting strange things have been happening to the
Allison family. Many of the dishes Mrs. Allison owns have been cracking
for some unknown reason. "It's been about two months ago that I put a
couple of goblets up on that window and the next morning they had cracked
right around the bottom." These cracks are circular in shape and no one
knows what has been causing this to happen for the past seven years.

When she first moved into the house she often saw a large cat-like
animal on the premises. "It was about three feet high and about three and
a half feet long," she told me. It would sit out in the driveway. Once
after a rain the family found three-inch footprints in the driveway and
claw marks one-half-inch deep and six inches long in a tree near the house.

8   Occupant

Above: Object seen by Mrs. Allison and son, Bruce, in 1968.
Right: Object seen by Mrs. Allison, Bruce and her husband Summer of 1975.

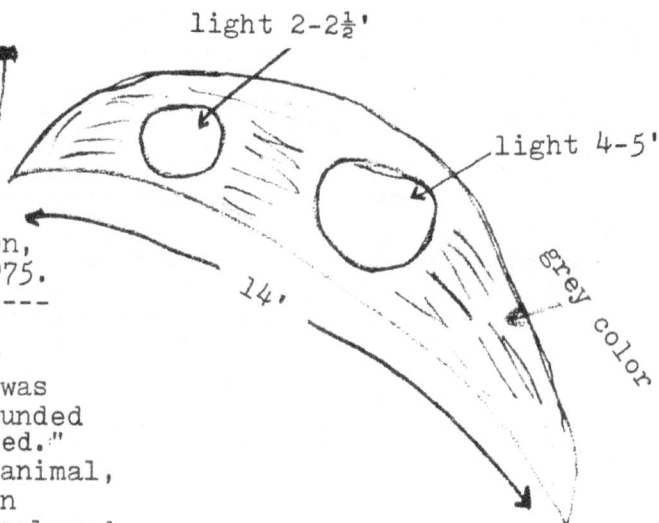

light 2-2½'
light 4-5'
grey color
14'

Both the Allison family and neighbors heard the creature. "My daughter woke up one night and it was growling and panting so loud it sounded as if it were at the foot of the bed." Nobody ever shot at or killed the animal, and a check with the nearest zoo in Cleveland, about 70 miles away, disclosed that no animal had escaped. Bruce told me that at his friend's house footprints had been found on top of the car. Af first they thought they had been made by their cat but the prints were much too large. "We found a big 'coon lying out in the woods. I don't know if someone had shot it and cut it open or what but it was just lying there." There was no blood or flesh, just the skin of the animal.

Ever since the creature sightings the Allisons have felt a strange presence in the woods next to their house. "I don't know what it was but it was something big that ran through the woods," Mrs. Allison said. "It was big enough to be a man, a big man. It would stand out in the woods and watch the house. All you could see was a black outline, but it definitely wasn't a bear." It was seen as recently as the past summer. One time when they entered the driveway Bruce said he saw the thing running through the woods. "It's not like a person, running through the woods -- you'll trip over stumps, branches and rocks. It ran so fast it didn't even look like it touched the ground. During the summer you could go out into the woods and see where it had been lying. Right before it started to get cold you could see this big spot. One night we heard our tomcat fighting with something and after that we never saw it again, but we can still feel its presence. It's out there!"

I asked Susan if she had seen the creature. She told me she had only heard it growling, but that her husband had experienced a strange happening. One morning while driving to work he was just leaving Salem Heights when suddenly he seemed to strike a very large man who seemed to jump in front of the car and put his hand up against the car to avoid being hit, and he felt a severe jolt. He stopped the car and jumped out but there was no victim in sight. There was a large dent in the fender and some black hairs sticking to it. The incident took place in 1971, she thought (In the summer of 1972 Ohio experienced a rash of "monster" or creature sightings).

The Allison family has continued to experience UFO sightings. About a month ago (November -- G.B.) Susan and her husband had a sighting from their house. They watched some lights through the kitchen window. "They were going around in a circle and there were two smaller ones behind it," she said. The lights were green, red, yellow and amber. There were three lights, two small ones and one large one. Eventually the large light left with a small one and the other light remained behind. When an airplane approached it rose to avoid being seen by the plane. She observed the objects for about an hour and when she left one small object was still there.

Susan also had another sighting last summer on her way to Lisband. "We thought it was an airplane when it flew over the car although we heard no motor, and it appeared to land in a field. She still doesn't know what it was. It was about the size of a plane and red in color. The next day they went to the field to investigate but found nothing.

One night the past summer Mrs. Allison was driving down Brooklyn Street in Salem with her son and husband. Suddenly they noticed a large copper-colored object following their car. As they turned up Third Street "it turned also and came right along with the car. We're lucky we didn't get hit, for it was about fifteen feet above the car. It was huge -- it must have been fourteen feet long!" This sighting lasted for about 10 minutes.

Bruce also experienced another sighting the past summer. He and his brother-in-law were at Cold Run Lake Park camping when they saw a light. "It came right down at us, then it stopped and looked as if it went down behind some trees. It looked like a street light, though a little duller."

(Mark Swift, 404 Niles-Vienna Ave., Vienna, O 44473, is Ohio representative for S.A.U.C.E.R.S. He is now away from home in medical school and may not receive and answer mail promptly until summer vacation)

DR. BERNARD IS ALIVE AND WELL! For some years we were under the impression that Dr. Raymond Bernard had met with an accident or foul play while exploring Brazilian jungles for cavern entrances to what he believed to be an Inner Earth. All communications stopped, and we presumed him dead. "Bernard" is the writing pseudonym of Walter Seigmeister, though the "Dr." part is real, representing a Ph. D. from Columbia University. Like a bolt out of the blue we received the following letter from Dr. Charles T. Turley, of Puerto Rico:

Dear Mr. Barker:

I write to you at the request of Walter Seigmeister. He is alive and in excellent health. I just met with him last week here in P.R.

He comes to see me often from his present home in Masars II, a colony in Agharta. I have learned many amazing things from both him and his friends from the interior of our Earth. I plan to travel to live with him there very soon and he asked me to contact you to arrange a meeting with him. Sincerely yours, Charles T. Turley.

(We are following this up and hope to report on it next Newsletter)

FOLLOW-UP ON THE WALTONS: THE MUNDO MONITOR (23084 Brookforest Rd., Novi, Mich. 48050) has some additional description of Travis Walton's abductors (Reported in Our No. 3). The #17 issue (Jan. '76) gleans the following from ACQUARIOUS VIEWPOINT of London and THE NATIONAL ENQUIRER.

Travis, these reports state, felt a terrible pain in his chest when he rose up into the ship. He awakened in what seemed to be a hospital, lying on a table on his back with figures standing over him. "It was weird. They weren't human -- they were creatures. They looked like well-developed fetuses to me. They were about 5 Ft. tall and wore tight-fitting tan/brown robes. Their skin was like a mushroom and they had no clear features. They made no sound. Their faces had no texture or color, and there was no hair. Their foreheads were domed and their eyes were very large. They had long fingers but no fingernails.

"I panicked and jumped up, knocking a clear plastic tray that was lying on my chest to the floor. I grabbed a transparent tube and tried to smash it, to use as a weapon, but it wouldn't break! I was knocked out again and when I awoke I was lying on the pavement about a quarter of a mile from Heber (Arizona)."

Some professional opinions about the Walton case:

Dr. James Harder, Prof. of Engineering, University of California: "This is the first abduction I know of that was witnessed by other people."

Dr. Howard Kandell, Arizona physician: "His physical condition was not that of a man who had been wandering about the woods for five days. There was a small puncture wound on the inside of his right arm, the kind you get from a blood test."

Letters

Dr. J. Allen Hynek, Director, Center for UFO Studies, Northfield, Il. 60093

Dear Dr. Hynek:

Thanks so much for the recent issue of the News Bulletin. The two news notes which stirred me into action were the notice concerning Vallee's paper at the AIAA meeting and the review of the Invisible College. Over the last 30 years I have personally collected and analyzed practically all published UFO data and have also interviewed dozens of individuals who have either seen UFO's or even have contacted UFO's. This has come to represent an enormous pile of data which coupled with psychic phenomena research is almost overwhelming. I have set out to reread and reconsider all this data as a whole. A short time ago I gave a talk, at a UFO meet in Tampa, Florida, in which UFO data and the data of psychic phenomena were compared item by item. It was obvious that we are not dealing with two separate clusters of information but rather we are dealing with a single assemblage of information accidentally categorized as being separate.

The whole reason for rereading all this data is to make sure that a working model of the UFO phenomena I believe to be true will be sustained by the data; I frankly believe it can be sustained.

The working model in question is quite unconventional and requires the acceptance of several complicated assumptions. Now, the assumptions are well within available concepts in Western Civilization although they have occupied a very minor position in scientific circles but nevertheless they are still intellectually viable. Well, here is the model:

UFO phenomena is a contrived paranormal event created for the benefit of the viewer with a specific stimulus content. This phenomena is a show-and-tell device precisely geared to the culture to which it is presented.

Note that all historical UFO sightings are always just slightly advanced for the viewers of the time. Medieval sightings were of a fully rigged sailing ship sailing along in the sky! 1897 sightings looked like a Victorian science fiction book illustration and the crews were all reported as being dressed properly for 1890. Current sightings are "space ships" with astronauts as pilots dressed in space suits. Obviously neither a sailing ship fully rigged nor a Jules Verne ship could possibly travel through interplanetary space in those forms from another planet to the earth and back. They all were here in physical form to be sure and were reported as such but that they did not get here in that form by flying here.

This display is intentional and is a part of a controlled program of cultural diffusion of special forms of information into current earth civilizations. The information is, however, in coded form! It is not obvious at all but is mixed in with considerable "noise." Not to be melodramatic but Toynbee has amply demonstrated that cultural advancement periodically is based on the productivity of a small number of creative people who are able to pick the signal out of the noise and come up with new conceptual patterns as described by Sorokin and Kroeber. It would appear that the last quarter of this century is such a time and perhaps your Invisible College may be that group who can decode the signal and thereby extract the key information. I hope they can do this before the Russians do it. The coded data in fact contains considerable information in the fields of technology, culture, philosophy, religion and sociology.

To paraphrase McLuhan the phenomena is the message the whole pattern must be considered as a total thing and not examined in a Spencerian fashion. If a piecemeal approach is used the total pattern will be lost with a resulting loss of information.

The rest of the model is built around the proposals put forward as early as 1947 by the discussants in the Mark Probert group in California. I keep coming back to these ideas because they simply do in fact explain details of the UFO phenomena.

Vide: The Coming of the Guardians, BSRA Vista, Ca., 1954, Seance Reports and Transcripts 1945-1960, BSRA Vista, Ca., Round Robin 1950-1960, BSRA, Vista, Ca.

This model is also found scattered around in a large part of published UFO data especially in contactee reports (most of which seem to be true, the ones I have investigated do have a ring of truth about them). Now the ETI model which is an extrapolation of our civilization fails to account for either paranormal phenomena or for the reported engineering designs, while the continuous violation of the known laws of physics and aero-dynamics eliminates the simple mechanical model of UFOs. The obvious limitations imposed on the use of a space vehicle of a mechanical sort by the sheer distance between solar systems again excludes the jet or ion driven space ship as a possible model.

The model that does appear to fit the data is incredible enough, the one which is constructed around the concept of a multidemensional universe which contains technically advanced civilizations some of which have reached the capability of multidimensional travel. This travel is a space time phenomena where a change of frequency is equivalent to an instant change in location, i.e., they dematerialize "there" and materialize "here". No distance or travel time is involved. Once here the ship or vehicle operates as a physical object in our dimension. It can violate the laws of physics by partially dematerializing, its physical appearance is determined by its mission not by any engineering demands and the crew may appear either as themselves or as manifesting a contrived appearance again depending on the mission.

It would appear that what is considered as a change in frequency is that matter comprising other dimensions varies from our matter in that the distance from the electron shells to the nucleus is much lesser there than here. In a sense their matter is more "dense" than our matter is so they expand their matter to materialize here and must hold it in this abnormal state in order to remain here. To return to their place they relax their energy field and immediately return. This difference in matter allows our mutual dimensions to normally coexist without interference except in some rare cases where a sort of splash-over takes place during which people and objects may appear or disappear suddenly.

The general cultural impact of the UFO pehnomena through its persistence and deliberate performances has been to create a knowledge revolution of a dramatic sort in the general population. This gives the creative minority a really favorable social climate in which to work. In a sense the phenomena has created a demand for new ideas -- now someone has to come up with them.

I have worked these ideas out in considerable detail and the more the concept is expanded the more it fits. You know the real problem in theory construction is timidity. We are all too often reluctant to move boldly into new domains and thus are unable to come to grips with intellectually explosive phenomena.

With the very best of personal regards.

J. H. Bruening, Department of Sociology and Anthropology, The University of Mississippi, College of Liberal Arts, University, Mississippi

Left: Martian and Vegetable Girl Friend, a tongue-in-cheek drawing by Dr. Donald H. Menzel. Many Menzel critics do not know that beneath his somewhat severe attacks on "saucer reality," he possesses a remarkable sense of humor. We have personally admired him for the time we know he has taken to religiously answer letters in detail, particularly those from young students and saucer fans. This drawing, reprinted from a humorous article, "Meet the Martians," which appeared in the Winter, 1965, issue of The Graduate Journal suffers from poor photographic reproduction here.

January 6, 1976

Dear Gray:

Thank you for your note and the January newsletter. I have no particular comments on the contactee cases. I wonder what you really think.

As for the "MEN IN BLACK", don't you really mean "MEN IN GREY"?

I appreciate your kind words about my "enormous contributions to saucer research." However, I have no idea what you mean by the statement: "But of course Menzel makes the terrible blunder of trying to explain all sightings with his system, and it doesn't work." In the first place, I have never claimed to have a "system," although certain ufologists imply that I try to explain all sightings in terms of meteorological optics, especially sundogs and mirages. That is absolute nonsense, and you know it!

I have listed more than 100 different kinds of phenomena that can be or have been identified as UFO's. I have searched most carefully for a "real honest-to-goodness saucer," but have failed to find a single one. I have challenged quite a few ufologists to present me with a dozen specific cases, which in their opinion cannot be solved by natural phenomena. Most of them failed to come up with a single convincing sighting. Others drag out the old cases that cannot be substantiated in any way or else have obviously simple explanations. Why don't you try it?

Thank you for your kind comments about my paintings of Martians, a combination of water color and India ink. You may be interested to know that I have four hanging in the Air and Space Museum of the Smithsonian Institution in Washington, D.C., at their invitation, of course. I am still doing some painting, in case one of your readers should be interested in acquiring one. The price is $100 and, you may be interested to know that Jim Moseley recently acquired one.

Finally, may I make a suggestion concerning your "very extensive private collection." The American Philosophical Society would be delighted to have it. I gave them my collection and they have since received the complete files of the late Edward U. Condon. Phil Klass has also given them some of his files. They feel--and I agree--that at least one major library should try to assemble in one place as much as possible of the data accumulated on the subject of flying saucers during the last quarter of a century and more. They will not only be glad to have your collection, I know. They will give you an evaluation for it, for income tax purposes. Your collection would be an extremely interesting supplement to those they already have. I am, therefore, sending a copy of my letter to you to their Librarian, Dr. Whitfield Bell, American Philosophical Society,

105 South Fifth Street, Philadelphia, Pa. 19106. You might publish this notice in your next newsletter, with the suggestion that other collectors, tired of their pursuit, may wish to make this donation.

You may be interested to know that I have just sent to the publishers, Doubleday, the manuscript of a new book, FLYING SAUCERS DOWN TO EARTH, with co-author Dr. Ernest Taves, a psychologist-psychiatrist-psychoanalyst. This book contains a great deal of new material on various cases, including a newly discovered form of optical illusion, which clearly accounts for a number of sightings.

You are free to use any or all of the above. Meanwhile, my best personal regards and best wishes for a Happy New Year.

Cordially yours, Donald H. Menzel

Center for Astrophysics, 60 Garden Street, Cambridge, Massachusetts 02138

Dear Donald:

Thank you for replying and commenting on my remarks about you in the Newsletter. I stand corrected in my statement that you try to explain all sightings and that you have a system. I do hope that more saucer buffs will take you up on your offer to examine their cases.

I hope your publisher can get me proofs of Flying Saucers Down to Earth well in advance of publication so that I can see that it is reviewed competently and fairly here and perhaps elsewhere. I am happy to learn that you are still writing for the lay press. In the past your books, public appearances and statements have provided a contrasting view to the reams of material written in support of the extraterrestrial hypothesis. If you have read the current book review section or the book itself, you will know that Vallee, an honest-to-goodness scientist, has abandoned the ET explanation, and definitely is now in the "4-D" camp. Hynek himself is getting "spookier" every day. With this sort of treatment of the UFO phenomena these boys may be eluding your surveillance by retreating into "inner space." With the abandonment of the ET explanation, and with the "4-D" theories chipping into the bulwarks of the so-called "UFO Establishment," your councils may be even more greatly in need to provide caution and balance.

Thanks for your information on the collection being acquired by the American Philosophical Society. This would seem to be a most appropriate agency to receive collection donations. Your tip on the income tax angle is well taken, though I wish I were in need of such a deduction -- my poor mouth matches my poor pocketbook.

Jim Moseley tells me that he is enjoying the painting he acquired from you recently. Congratulations on your representation at the Smithsonian. I hope some of my readers will get in touch with you at the address above about acquisitions of your paintings.

In regard to the contactees, you wonder what I "really think." I wish I could form a firm conclusion, but I have not. As to the MIB, I don't understand your reference to "men in grey," unless the agents of the C blank blank usually dress in grey suits.

Hearing from you is always enlightening and pleasurable.

Kindest regards,
Gray

RANDOM THOUGHTS(?) TO FILL UP A PAGE: In regard to Pete Bruening's letter to Hynek, it might be productive to dig out and re-read Meade Layne's writings about the Mark Probert controls. This material is the saucer-age forerunner of all the current mat and demat stuff. If Middle Ufologists examine or re-examine these theories they may be convinced, as am I, that the Yada was not a crock of Shi'ite.

Threeish of this Newsletter is still available at $1.00 per copy. For those of you who have just come in, our Nos. 1 and 2 were just single page affairs. The first one was mainly an ad blurb, and No. 2 was a weirdie about MIB outside our office. No charge for them if you really want them.

14   IN AND OUT OF ZINES

MEET THE LORDS (The Awareness Research Foundation, Inc., Bx 610143,
North Miami, Fla. Single Copy $1, 12 ish $10) is a lively 8½ x 11" 4 pp
3 col. typescript UFO/Psychic zine. Typical ish contains an account by
Edward M. Palmer, Ms. D., Ph. D. of his ride in a spacecraft to the moon.
On the night of Nov. 26, 1969, Dr. Palmer walked out of his home into the
back patio where he saw a large 50-ft. disc. He was levitated into the
craft where he sat beside the pilot in a reclining chair.

"As we came close to the Moon we headed straight toward a large
crater which appeared to have water in it; we went right down into the water,
into the crater and came in through a tunnel, and then started up, coming
to the surface of the water, and there was a port, similar to those we
have on our river banks."

Dr. Palmer was ushered into a large building "where a lot of activity
was taking place. They were making small electrical devices, some looked
like our electrical motors and generators. I was taken to the foreman of
the shop and introduced to him. His name was Mr. Hamilton. He was an
electrical engineer. He said that he came from Los Angeles, California,
and was very excited when I said I was from Portland, Oregon, and that I
had been to Los Angeles.....Shortly my pilot said we must return to Earth
now, so we went back to the ship, and when in the ship I said: 'How about
the water?' He said that it is a sort of a valve we go in and out of
without changing the temperature sometimes, and that way we can control our
temperature inside."

Zine contains regular contributions by Raymond Fowler, who is the
father of better known Raymond E. Fowler, author of UFOs Interplanetary
Visitors (Foreword by J. Allen Hynek) (Exposition Press, Jericho, NY,
1974, $8.50). In an article, "With Angels In a War Zone," the elder
Fowler tells of the death of an elderly friend named "Mac," who returned
in spirit body and took Fowler temporarily from his physical body to a
space ship. This was during World War II, and "Mac" had joined a group of
spirits who helped wounded and dying soldiers in Europe, thus fulfilling
his earthly unrealized dream of becoming a physician. Not only was the
spirit group "assisting" in the medical treatments but were "lifting up
the spirits of those whose physical bodies had been slaughtered, and these
spirits were taken to other planes and dimensions according to the uses
that they had made of their lives before becoming involved in the war."
The younger Fowler is a scientific associate for the Center For UFO
Studies in Northfield, Ill. We should mention that LORDS is edited by
Helen I. Hoag.

"What imagination...wish I
had stuff like this when I
was a kid!"

CONFIDENTIAL NEWSLETTER of the National
Investigations Committee on UFOs (7970 Woodman Ave.,
Van Nuys, Ca 91402, $15 per yr domestic, $20 For.)
Edited by Frank E. Stranges, long associated with
the UFO field. Vol. 7, No. 5 announces production
on a forthcoming film by Stranges, who did the
saucer film, Phenomena 7.7. This ish contains
about 3½ pp of UFO news, rest ads, including one
on The Ideal Lift and Skin Care Program.

VISIONS (Jesiam Centre, 5 Tennyson St.,
Kew, 3101, Victoria, Australia, 50¢ per ish) is a
7-8 pp offset pub containing "The master's messages
given in telepathic impression to his Followers in
Fulfilment of Acts 2:17." In the Xmas '75 ish,
David, speaking on Christmas and the coming year,
promises that the New Year will begin a special
7-year cycle in which the cosmic masters of the
hierarchy will "raise the atomic vibration of all
on Earth to the 4th density of Venus." Same commu-
nicator also warns of the "dark forces of Samanah,
(who) will launch their attack........"

OMEGA MAGAZINE AND DIRECTORY (Bx 2145, Scottsdale, Az. 85252, (602) 947-7984, 12 ish Dom. $4, For. $6) is a psychic-oriented tabloid-size 12-pager, though the 12/75 ish features UFO cover art and a story on the Walton abduction. Primarily directed toward Arizona readers, its Organization Directory lists more than 90 study groups and churches, from the A.A.S. Thaumaturgy Study Group to Valley Unitarian Universalist Church. This no. includes articles on Meditation, Astrosonics, Astrology, Predictions and Wicca.

U.F.O. HOTLINE (3355 Lakeshore Drive, Muskegon, Mich 49441 (616) 755-2305, 8 ish (yrly) $5) This 8½ x 11" typescript offset zine is published by Clifford R. Stenberg, another true supporter of Middle Ufology. Ish No. 2 is

"...and then I told the witch doctor to go screw himself."

8 pages and contains much good material, including a good letters section. Thish ish also has a fascinating article on artifacts left by the Dropa in a Chinese cavern, and another about a strange stone, containing the remains of tiny "spacemen" discovered in 1968 by Mr. and Mrs. Melvin Gray near Louisville, Ky. The stone was subjected to a 10-month study by Buffard Ratliff, director of the now defunct National UFO Research and Investigations Committee, who lectured widely about it. I don't know whether to thank Editor Stenberg or to give him two knocks on the head, but encouragement by himself (and a few other active researchers) led me to get back into zine publishing.

Another voiceferous spokesman for Middle Ufology, Dennis Pilichis, publishes PAGE RESEARCH LIBRARY NEWSLETTER (6707 Colgate Ave., Cleveland, O. 44102, 4 ish $1) which is a palatable potpourri of saucers and other denizens of the borderland of establishment science. No 12 contains listings of books, comments on other zines, a bleeding statue and dire predictions of the BVM (Blessed Virgin Mary -- see Book Review -- Greenfield, please add to Ufology terms); a rather technical discussion of Kirlian photography and a generous serving of Nessie. First time we have seen this journal, and this one, like the others we have been receiving in exchange for our rag #3 which we sent out to almost everybody, is very good. We hope Dennis never tries to slick this one up in an effort to become a SKYLOOK.

Which brings us to SKYLOOK (26 Edgewood Drive, Quincey, Il 62301, Monthly $8 yr, $9 For. Sample 75¢.) While this zine is getting slicker, there is some suggestion that it is succumbing to a common saucerian syndrome: the November ish reached me on January 7th, and the Editor's Column promises that "very quickly now we will be sending out the December issue." Veterans such as Moseley, Steinberg, Beckley, Barker and the like know that this syndrome is rarely cured and that the terminus is a sad affair known as "F-O-L-D-I-N-G." We sympathize with editor Dwight Connelly, whose father suffered an accident. Mrs. Connelly, who is credited with doing much of the nitty gritty work at SKYLOOK headquarters, was helping out at his father's residence and the mail was piling up. The absence of the business manager further was complicating things.

For the average buff and collector the November ish is quite marvelous. It is in the form of a calendar punched for hanging, with a classic saucer case, illustrated with a large photo or drawing, heading each month. Unlike the Raymond's Pills calendar one may still obtain in country stores,

with its weather prediction printed in the square with each day, the
SKYLOOK calendar notes saucerevents that happened on particular days (we
learn that on March 21, 1974, Maximiliano Iglesias Sanchez saw three
grounded spacecraft with humanoids taking soil samples near Horcajo,
Spain). A majority of the day squares are still blank, and the most of
these probably could be filled in if one had access to a computerized
collection that could spew out sighting information by months and days.
John Keel's "Wednesday phenomenon" doesn't fare well in the calendar:
the most sightings in the MUFON calendar occur on Monday and Thursday
(nine each) with Wednesday, along with Tuesday, Friday and Saturday,
boasting only seven sightings each. Sunday is the "worst" day with five.
But of course MUFON doesn't claim the calendar is statistically sound, and
jesting aside, it represents a great deal of work and is a very nice item.
To myself, suffering a constant identity crisis, the calendar will occupy
a prominent place in my living room, a constant reassurance that the saucers
are real. It will replace my Technicolor masterpiece, "Twelve International
Beauties," which expired on Dec. 31, but the saucer illustrations, whatever
they may lack in exposed flesh, are archetypal and, as always, are grossly
symbolic in a phallic sense.

Richard Hall's "Recapping and Commenting" occupies most of one of
the two pages of editorial matter (unfortunately removed this from
the back cover), and he is complaining in his Item No. (5) that "Crackpot
and self-aggrandizing speakers and writers still are confusing the issues."
He then, in his Item No. (6) gives us the comforting observation that
"Funds are not available, especially in the midst of rampant inflation,
to support the scientific groups."

If you don't subscribe to SKYLOOK, this November (calendar) ish
would be well worth your sending for as a sample, though it is priced at
$1.00. Better send off right away for this is certain to sell out
quickly.

SKYLOOK has obtained a Second Class Postage Permit, which means
that like the bigger magazines, they can mail at a cheap, subsidized
postal rate. Their Statement of Ownership, Management and Circulation
(as required by law) appearing in the October issue, indicates that the
actual number of copies published nearest to filing date was 1450. Mail
subscriptions during the previous 12 month averaged 1250. We don't know
NICAP's nor APRO's circulations but we suspect SKYLOOK's is greater, and
that it is surpassed only by Ray Palmer's FLYING SAUCERS, with a circulation averaging 4300 reported in the March, 1975, issue.

WHILE FILING OLD ZINES, I came across a defunct one called
SAUCERITUS (a great title that should be revived, and while we're on this,
how about one named UFORIA or STENDEC?) which is not appropriate to review
here but in which I spotted an item I had been looking for (I told you
so Greenfield!).

I knew that a man named Fred Crisman had been summoned to testify
in the trial of Clay Shaw, who was acquitted for an alleged conspiracy
to kill John Kennedy, but who was ruined in the process, financially,
personally and physically. I could never find the item in clippings I
had on the trial (I was into the Conspiracy Theory at the time) and assumed
it must involve some Crisman other than the one involved in the Tacoma
Affair back in 1947 (See Arnold and Palmer, The Coming of the Saucers,
privately published by Palmer in 1952).

According to this New Orleans UPI story in the Nov. 22, 1968, ish
of The Arkansas Gazette, "A Tacoma, Wash., radio announcer who said he
had nothing to tell District Attorney Jim Garrison about the assassination
of President John F. Kennedy went before the Orleans Parish Grand Jury
Thursday. Fred Lee Crisman, 47, was accompanied by his attorney......Crisman
told newsmen, however, that he knew Thomas Beckham, an Omaha, Neb. evan-
gelist, who testified in the Garrison investigation earlier this year."

No doubt this is the same Crisman, and we will leave this matter
for your speculation.

KOLLECTOR'S KORNER

All right, folks, you've seen the medicine show, so now let's talk some BU$INE$$. Here's a continuation of last month's Korner, consisting of very scarce and relatively scarce saucer items that likely will appreciate in value as collectors' items. Include 20¢ per item for pp unless stated.

NEW YORK'S FIRST FLYING SAUCER CONVENTION. This is a transcript of lectures made at Jim Moseley's controversial 1967 Con. Some say it was the greatest ever held, though members of the UFO Establishment have called it a "circus" -- and the late Edmund U. Condon was never quite forgiven for attending it in person! Transcripts of lectures by Dr. Frank Stranges, actor Roy Thinnes, John Keel, Gray Barker, The Amazing Randi, Ivan T. Sanderson, Long John Nebel (with Vi-Venus, an alleged Venusian living here on Earth), Howard Menger, others. 106 pp. We have only a few. $25.00

SAUCERS SPACE & SCIENCE, the great zine edited by Gene Duplantier (no longer pubbed). 8½ x 11" offset. Each ish contains dramatic sightings, but the outstanding feature is the layout and art work by Duplantier, a gifted illustrator. Issues available: #'s 52, 53, 54, 56, 57, 58, 59, 60, 61, 63, 64. $2.00 ea.

FATE MAGAZINE of 1960's each containing UFO article, our select.$1.00

AIDS TO IDENTIFICATION OF FLYING OBJECTS. 36-pp (Aprox 4x5") booklet published 1968 by Dept. of Defense. Stresses natural phenomena origin of UFOs but does contain valuable tips on identifying knowns. Well illustrated, and has a rather surprising bibliography that includes Flying Saucers In the Bible. $2.00

FROM OUTER SPACE TO YOU, large Tabloid ish of Psychic Observer (8/25-59) containing the entire story from the Menger Book, including all the photos printed same size (or larger) as in the orig. OP book.$2.00.

FROM OUTER SPACE TO YOU by Menger foreign editions: LES HOMES DE L' ESPACE (large hard cover size but paper bound) in French; AUS DEM WELTRAUM ZU EUCH (hard cover in German), $10.00 each.

TIME OF THE END by Laura Mundo, rare OP tabloid size booklet, 34 pp typeset, on newsprint and getting yellow. Long OP $2.00

"One-sheet" movie poster for display at theatre, MYSTERIES FROM BEYOND EARTH, multi-colored, $3.00.

"YOUNG FRANKENSTEIN" 16mm sound TV spots, 60 Sec. $2.00, 30 Sec 75¢

SAUCERIAN BULLETIN, Vol. 4, No. 1, May, 1959, includes story on Al Bender with picture, and five pages of Monguzzi photos. 36pp. $2.00

THE FLYING SAUCER AS I SAW IT, published by Kenneth Arnold in 1950. Autographed. 9x12, 16 pp beautifully printed in sepia. Contains stat of letter to Arnold from wife of Frank Brown, who died in plane crash at Tacoma, Wn, while investigating the "Tacoma Affair." Also letter to Arnold from George F. Gorman, apologizing how security has been clamped down on his "saucer chase." Have seen only one copy of this in 25 years and it is yours for $50.00.

THE SAUCER PEOPLE by Ronald G. Garver, privately printed, hard cover book (Fiction). $5.00.

LARGE BOLT FROM WRECKAGE OF SILVER BRIDGE. $25.00. Include street address since this will be shipped UPS charges collect.

Paperbacks by Daniel W. Fry: STEPS TO THE STARS, $3.00; ATOMS, GALAXIES & UNDERSTANDING, $3.00.

SAUCER NEWS Vol. 11, No. 4, Whole No 58 12/64. This ish is annotated in pencil throughout by editor James Moseley, expressing what he REALLY thinks about the contents. Some of the comments are very humorous. For instance, adjacent to one advertisement: "This dam deadbeat has not paid for the ad!" $25.00.

NEXUS pubbed by August C. Roberts and Dominick C. Lucchesi. One-shot, and precursor to the NEXUS title which began SAUCER NEWS. 8pp about 4x5" ditto, with cover by Lucchesi. $25.00

Many items last bulletin still not sold. If in doubt send letter asking to reserve. Money refunded if you order and item sold out.

KEEL'S SUPERSPECTRUM

(See Book Review) Hold graph close to eyes and concentrate on the center of the Superspectrum for 30 seconds. Either this or reading Keel's EIGHTH TOWER may draw you into a world outside yourself.

From
Saucerian Press, Inc.
Box 2228
Clarksburg, WV 26301
U.S. Planet Earth

THIRD CLASS MAIL

Postperson, please deliver to:

Where there is no vision
the people perish.
        --Proverbs, 29:18

www.ingramcontent.com/pod-product-compliance
Lightning Source LLC
Chambersburg PA
CBHW050415110426
42812CB00006BA/1897